THE AGE OF BLISS

PROPHET
MUHAMMAD ﷺ

MUSTAFA ERDOĞAN

NEW JERSEY • LONDON • FRANKFURT • CAIRO • JAKARTA

TUGHRA
BOOKS

New Jersey

Translated by Türker Çiftçi
Published by Tughra Books
335 Clifton Ave., Clifton,
NJ, 07011, USA
www.tughrabooks.com

Library of Congress Cataloging-in-Publication Data

Erdogan, Mustafa.
[Hazreti Muhammed. English]
Prophet Muhammad : the beloved messenger of Allah / Mustafa Erdogan.
pages cm
ISBN 978-1-59784-382-9 (alk. paper)
1. Muhammad, Prophet, -632–Biography. I. Title.
BP75.27.E7313 2014
297.6'3–dc23
[B] 2014036469

ISBN: 978-1-59784-382-9

TABLE OF CONTENTS

A Star Was Born

*I*t was the month of April, in the year 571. One Monday morning, an extraordinary radiance covered the east and the west.

That day, strange things happened one after the other. Idols at the Ka'ba toppled over and fell onto the floor. The people of Mecca were amazed at this. How could idols that had been fixated fall over?

A terrifying tremor was happening in Persia (present-day Iran), many kilometers away from Mecca. King Chosroes jumped out of his bed. He tried to understand what was happening. With fear in their eyes, the guards explained, "Your Highness! Fourteen towers of the palace have collapsed!"

Less than a minute later, a wail of sorrow began in the streets of Persia, "The fire went out! The fire went out!" The Zoroastrian people couldn't believe this: the "holy fire" they had worshipped for a thousand years, which had never gone out, had suddenly died.

Another community was facing a strange case, too. The people of Sawah had seen their sacred lake suddenly dry up. The land had swallowed tons of water. The people of Sawah no longer had their "holy water." Nobody could make anything out of this.

In this Age of Ignorance, it was common but pitiful to see people considering the Divine blessings of fire or water "holy"—so holy they even worshipped them! The most pitiful and yet funny sight one could ever see was, however, the Meccan polytheists' worshipping of their handmade idols, attributing divinity to them!

Another amazing sign appearing that very night was the appearance of many shooting stars drawing arcs across the heavens. Indeed, those who watched the sky that night were surprised to see so many stars.

"Look, look there! Stars are falling one after another! This is an odd situation. If it goes on like this, there won't be any stars left in the sky!"

The next morning, the sun appeared from behind the mountains. There was liveliness in the house of Amina. A woman came running up to Abdul Muttalib, who was near the Ka'ba, and said: "Good tidings to you. You have a grandson!"

Joy covered Abdul Muttalib's face. He went straight home, and he embraced the orphan of his dead son, Abdullah. What a beautiful baby he was! He was constantly smiling. Abdul Muttalib said, "This son of mine will definitely be an important person."

Amina told them of a dream she had when she got pregnant. In her dream, somebody said, "Know that you carry the blessing of the universe. When your baby is born, name him Muhammad, and don't tell further details of your dream to anyone." Thereupon, Amina gave the name Muhammad to her son.

Abdul Muttalib picked up his grandson and went straight to the Ka'ba. He prayed lengthily there, and thanked Glorious Allah. Then he returned and handed the baby to his mother.

His mother began to nurse the child. However, Amina didn't have any milk. A solution came to mind. Hamza ibn Abdul Muttalib's wet nurse,

Suwayba, was called. The baby was given to her, and he was nursed for the first time by this woman. Therefore, infant Muhammad became milk siblings with his own uncle, Hamza.

Wet Nurse

The sky was blue. There was nothing but a few small pleasant white clouds and the morning sun. The village of Banu Sa'd was preparing for a new day.

As the minutes went by, the activity at the land of Banu Sa'd was increasing. People were taking their camels, donkeys, and mules out of their stables.

An old camel was resting in the shade of the almost dry date orchard. The animal was noticeably skinny. Her ribs could be counted one by one, even from a distance.

The cry of a baby in a house close to the date orchard could be heard even in the street. A tired woman was trying to comfort the baby with lullabies. However the woman sang, the baby kept crying, raising its voice to a wail.

A stooping man with a pale face came out of the house sorrowful. He walked toward the camel in the date orchard. While he was getting dressed, he had murmured to himself, "How long will this famine last? Babies are hungry, mothers are hungry... If mothers can't find food to eat, how can they have milk?"

The man stopped next to the camel. He bent over and checked the animal's udders. His face clouded over. He turned back, went into the house, and said to the woman trying to comfort her crying baby, "No. There isn't even enough milk for you in the camel."

The woman's eyes ran over the man's helpless face, and said, "Milk whatever there is and bring it. Otherwise Abdullah won't keep quiet during the journey."

The man took a container, and went out to the camel. Too soon, he came back. He put the container, which had very little milk, on the fire. While they waited for the milk to warm up, he said, "We have to set off at once, Halima. Our neighbors have started to prepare their mounts already. We shouldn't fall behind. Otherwise we won't be able to find a child to nurse."

As the woman rocked her baby on her lap, she desperately asked, "What if we do find one, Harith? What could I nurse it with? Don't you see my milk isn't even enough for our own baby? The poor thing couldn't sleep all night because of hunger. Will the baby we take be in a situation different from this one?"

The man didn't reply for a while. The milk had warmed up. He put it in a bowl, handed it to the woman, and said: "Come on, drink it, Halima. Meanwhile, I will prepare the animals. Then we will set off."

As Harith went out, Halima took the bowl to her mouth.

Sometime later, the caravan set off. The villagers were heading towards Mecca, talking with each other. At one stage, a young woman looked back and called out, "Halima, you're falling behind."

Halima looked at the old donkey beneath her as if she was angry with it. Harith spurred the animal with the palm of his hand and said, "Come on, please."

The donkey shuddered, and shot ahead for a moment. But then it carried on walking its usual slow pace.

The rest of the villagers arrived in Mecca. Harith and Halima had fallen behind. By the time they entered the city, the others had visited each and every house. For wealthy Meccans would entrust their babies to the villagers who came, saying things like:

"Take good care of our baby. We want our children to grow up in the cool air of your plateau, not in the boiling heat of Mecca. Teach them our language properly. Do not worry about the cost of care. We will give more than you want, as long as you raise our child properly."

Those who came would say to them in a reassuring manner:

"Do not worry at all. We will treat your baby like our own baby. We will take care of them in the best way."

Harith and his wife Halima finally reached Mecca. Being late added to the tiredness of the journey, and they were disheartened. They had no hope of finding a rich family now. They knocked on the door of the first house they came to. The answer was as they expected: "We gave our baby to a family that came earlier."

They knocked on another door. The answer was the same. They didn't give up. They ran to another house. The scene they encountered was not encouraging. Everybody was giving the same answer.

Halima couldn't accept this. She was very tired. Her baby was growing heavier in her arms, so she gave him to her husband.

She said, "You wait for me here," and continued walking around. Passing near the Ka'ba, she noticed a respectable older man. For a reason she did not know, she stopped where she was. She looked carefully at the old man. The sweet old man was no one other than Abdul Muttalib. When he noticed Halima looking at him, he asked, "Who are you?"

Halima introduced herself and explained why she had come. With a smile on his face, Abdul Muttalib said, "O Halima, there is an orphan baby in my house. I offered him to your friends. Nobody wanted to be his wet nurse. Come, be his wet nurse. I hope that you will benefit from him."

Halima thought for a moment. She had come here for the children of wealthy families. If the child was an orphan, she wouldn't make much. How would they make a living? But there were no other children left in Mecca. She didn't want to go back empty-handed. She looked helplessly at Abdul Muttalib and said, "I shall ask my husband."

She went straight to Harith, told him the situation and said, "I couldn't find a child. I don't want to go back among my friends empty-handed, either. I'm going to take that baby!"

Harith bowed his head. There was nothing to do. With a faint hope that they would be better off one day somehow, he said, "It's up to you, Halima. Maybe Allah will give our house abundance for the sake of that orphan."

Halima hurried back and found Abdul Muttalib. She told him that she accepted the offer. Abdul Muttalib was very pleased. They started to walk toward the house together.

Amina welcomed them with a smile. Understanding that Halima was a wet nurse, Amina invited her in. As soon as Halima stepped into the house, she smelled something wonderful. As she looked around, she noticed the cradle in the corner. At that moment, she felt her heart leap. Excitedly, she walked towards the cradle. With every step, she was deeply inhaling the fragrance in the room.

When she reached the cradle, she knelt down. As she was reaching out to the child, she had strange feelings. Finally, she lifted the covering. There was a green blanket spread out under the tiny baby. And there was a white sheet on top of him. His face was so bright that Halima gazed at him in admiration. Amina, who was standing next to her, said, "His name is Muhammad."

Halima felt very peaceful. She stared at the beautiful baby almost without breathing or blinking. She couldn't resist, and picked up the baby. At that moment, the beautiful eyes of Muhammad opened. Halima's excitement doubled. She smiled at him with affection. The baby started to smile sweetly, too. Halima decided to try to nurse the baby then and there. As she guided her right breast to the rose-scented baby's lips, a concern surfaced in her. Would her milk come?

The baby had just begun to suckle when Halima shivered. She was shocked. With eyes wide open, she looked at the baby in her arms. Milk was flowing into the lovely baby's mouth.

Halima turned in confusion to Amina. But Amina was looking at her son. In her eyes, there was pain, the pain of the separation that was coming. She must have wondered how she was going to survive being apart from her child.

After nursing, Halima stood up. Saying farewell to Amina, she said, "Be sure I will take care of your son as well as my own baby."

Amina sent off her only child with tears in her eyes.

Halima returned to her husband with a smile on her face. Harith was tired of trying to comfort his son, who was constantly crying in his arms. He was startled when he noticed his wife's joy. When he saw the bright-faced baby in her arms, he understood why. He loved this sweet baby from the moment he saw him. He took a fancy to him at once.

They spent the night close to Mecca. Halima was nursing her son, Abdullah, and the future Seal of the Prophets, at the same time. Both babies drank milk to their hearts' content.

Once, Halima tried to change the places of the two babies. She took the infant Muhammad toward her left breast. But she encountered a surprising situation. The baby wouldn't nurse from that side. So Halima took him to the right side again, and he started to nurse.

For the first time in his young life, little Abdullah had enough milk, thanks to the abundance that came with his milk sibling. He slept soundly with a full stomach.

In the morning, Harith woke up. He went straight to the camel. When he came back to his wife a little later, he was puzzled. The old camel that had given very little milk until that day had become a milk fountain. He showed the container full of milk to Halima and said, "Halima, you brought a holy guest to us!"

Preparations were completed. They set off again to return home. Halima mounted the donkey with the two babies in her arms. The donkey that could hardly walk before was now as fast as lightning. In a short time, it made its way to the front of the caravan. Everyone they left behind was astonished. Harith and Halima knew the reason for it. The baby they carried with them wasn't an ordinary one.

Eventually they reached their home. From that day, Harith and his family lead a very peaceful, abundant life. Their animals were full when they returned from the meadows. The sheep fattened in a short time. They all began to give plenty of milk.

Neighbors noticed and scolded their shepherds, "What is the condition of our animals? Why are they skinny and why don't they give milk?"

"We swear we graze your animals in the best possible places," they replied.

"Halima's sheep are so fleshy! Milk is dripping from their udders. What sort of shepherds are you, anyway? From now on, you will graze our animals wherever Halima's shepherd grazes her animals! Our sheep should be like hers."

The shepherds were speechless. From that moment on, they went wherever Halima's shepherd took his flock. But nothing changed. Nobody but Harith and Halima could understand it.

Allah the Almighty was showering abundance on the house His Prophet was in.

Months went by. Little Muhammad grew fast. When he was two years old, Halima took him in her arms. She went straight to Mecca and there she found Amina. As agreed, she had brought the boy to give him back to his mother.

Amina was delighted beyond description when she saw her only son. She hugged him, and smelled him. Little Muhammad was also very joyful.

Abdul Muttalib came, as well. He was very happy to see his grandson, who had gone when he was only two months old, and was now two years old. He took him in his arms and played with him.

But Halima didn't want to be separated from her fosterling. This adorable child had brought happiness and abundance to their home. She looked at Amina and said, "Please give him to me for awhile more."

Amina didn't know what to say. Halima carried on talking, "I am afraid of him being infected by the plague outbreak in Mecca."

Amina looked at Halima, and then to her son. That terrible disease spreading in Mecca had been on her mind. She felt pain in her heart. Halima was waiting for an answer. Amina nodded as tears ran down her face. It meant, "All right, he can go with you."

That day, she kissed and smelled her baby again and again. At last, she handed him over to his wet nurse. Like two years before, she again sent off her darling in tears. Little Muhammad was going to the land of Banu Sa'd again.

The Heart Washed with Snow

The rose-scented Prophet was five years old. As usual, he was shepherding the flock with his milk sibling, Abdullah. They got carried away with their games. They felt tired, and sat under the shade of a date tree.

Abdullah couldn't help falling asleep. A little later, he awakened and looked around for his milk sibling. When he saw him being laid down by two men in a meadow, he panicked. He ran home screaming.

Halima came out of her house in a hurry. Her son was trying to tell her something, but in his fright he couldn't get the words out. He was pointing with one hand to the place where the sheep were.

He managed to say, "They slit Muhammad's chest."

When she heard this, Halima nearly fainted. Without waiting, she ran in the direction her son had pointed. When she found Muhammad, standing on his feet, she felt relief wash over her. She hugged him to her, and checked his body at the same time. Looking everywhere, she could find nothing wrong with him. But his face was pale. Halima's husband, Harith, came to them. He, too, hugged the boy, and asked, "What happened?"

Little Muhammad looked somewhat pale, and told the story. "Two men in white robes came and laid me down. They split my chest and took my heart out. Then they washed my heart with snow."

Harith took the boy by the hand and brought him home. The children started to play with each other again. Harith pulled his wife aside. In a faint voice he said, "I fear that something bad may happen to this child. It's best that we give him back to his family."

Halima didn't want to give beautiful Muhammad back to his mother yet, but this incident had made her rather anxious. Unwillingly, they took the boy to Amina.

A Mother's Sorrow

fter receiving her child from his wet nurse, Amina was very happy. Sometime later, she wished to visit her relatives in Medina. With her maidservant Umm Ayman, they got prepared quickly. One morning, they set off in the boiling heat of the desert with two camels. Muhammad was now six years old. He was very pleased by this trip. He was quietly making his way on his mother's lap.

Amina took this trip every year. She went to Medina to see family, and visit her husband's grave. On previous journeys, she was very joyful. But this year, she was in sorrow. The pain in her heart wasn't going away.

The guests came to the house of Nabigha, young Muhammad's cousin. Their camels knelt and rested in the courtyard of the house. A crowd of people was waiting for them there. The uncle of Muhammad welcomed them in to rest. However, Amina wanted to visit Abdullah's grave first.

The sorrowful mother cried to Allah, finding consolation in her bright-faced child. Young Muhammad lifted his palms and prayed for his father, too, almost as if he wanted to say, "Don't cry, mother!"

After staying in Medina for about a month, they started making preparations for their return. On the way back, Amina fell ill and they stopped to rest at the village of Abwa. Amina was in pain, and was too ill to continue the trip. Perhaps she was sad because she knew she was going to leave her son alone. She turned to her son and spoke to him one last time.

"May Allah make you glorious and perpetual. If what I saw in my dream (when I was pregnant) is true, you will be a Prophet sent to humankind by Allah—the One of Majesty and Grace, in order to teach them what is *halal* and *haram*, what is permitted and forbidden. Allah will protect and withhold you from idolatry." After these words, she passed away.

After his mother's death, little Muhammad returned to Mecca with Umm Ayman, who was later described by the Messenger of Allah as "A mother to me after my mother." Of course, Allah the Almighty didn't abandon the rose-scented boy. First his grandfather, Abdul Muttalib, and then his uncle, Abu Talib, safeguarded him.

Separations

Abdul Muttalib took his grandson, who was left without a father or mother, into his house. He showed more love and compassion to the boy than he had shown to his own sons.

Beautiful Muhammad never left his grandfather's side. Even when Abdul Muttalib was sleeping, he freely went in and out of the room. When none of his sons were permitted to sit on his cushions in the shade of the Ka'ba, he did whenever he wanted.

When a man he didn't know took him off the cushion one day, he began to cry. His grandfather stood up and looked in the direction of the sound, and asked those who were with him, "Why is my son crying?"

They replied, "Someone took him off the cushion." Abdul Muttalib said, "Let my son sit there. He has an honor that nobody else can reach."

As the days went by, his grandfather never let him feel the absence of his parents.

At the age of eighty-two, Abdul Muttalib came down with an illness. When he knew he was going to die, he gathered his sons around him. He commanded them to take good care of the beautiful Muhammad, who would be left behind. Zubayr and Abu Talib drew straws to see who would take Muhammad into his home. Abu Talib won. The serene and lovely child who had lost his parents, and now his grandfather, would be protected by his uncle Abu Talib.

Abu Talib had nothing but a few milk-giving camels. His family was large, too. He was having trouble making a living. To break free of these troubles, Abu Talib decided to join the trade caravan that was going to go to Damascus. Lovely Muhammad had hopes for this trip. Would his uncle choose to bring him?

Camels were prepared; the trip was going to begin. All of Abu Talib's children were waiting to say farewell to their father. Abu Talib approached his nephew, who was on the verge of tears, and asked, "Do you want to come?"

Young Muhammad had set his heart on it. But his other uncles didn't want him to go; they worried he would fall ill on the long trip. Upon hearing their objections, the boy began to cry.

Abu Talib was moved by his tears, and asked, "Are you crying because I'm leaving you behind?"

Through his tears, the boy said, "Yes." He held the rein of his uncle's camel. "O uncle, who are you leaving me with? I have no father, nor mother."

His uncle couldn't resist these sincere, plaintive words.

He said, "By Allah, I will take you with me, and I will never leave you." He took his young nephew with him and joined the caravan.

Muhammad, who was now twelve years old, therefore, set off for Damascus with his uncle.

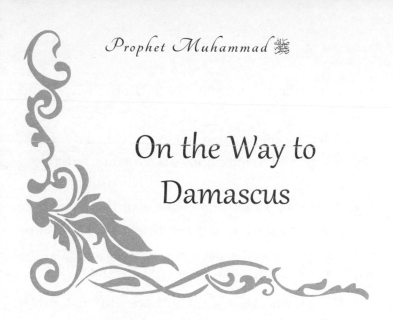

On the Way to Damascus

a warm wind blew in through the open window of the monastery. The monk Bahira sat at a small table inside. Just then, he closed the book he was reading. Then he stood up to drink some water. He approached the window and looked at the desert. There was nothing but date trees. There was only the desert.

A shepherd was pulling water from a well for his sheep. The monk squinted, and looked again at the horizon. A caravan appeared among the sand dunes. The monk watched the caravan for awhile, and then went outdoors to the well. The other monks ran to his side. They pulled water from the well and offered it to Bahira.

At the moment when his foot touched the steps, Bahira snapped to attention. The distant caravan had come into focus, and the individuals could be seen. But there was something odd about the vision. He delayed going back to his room and leaned against the wall. He studied the caravan for a long while. As it got closer, the monk's curiosity grew.

The caravan took a break under the date trees. The trees bent over it, as if they were bowing toward the caravan, as if they were greeting it.

The monk Bahira grew more puzzled. He called a novice monk, Ahbar, over to him. He gestured to the well and said, "I wonder where this caravan is coming from." Ahbar looked from the monk to the caravan, and said, "I don't know. It could be coming from Mecca." Bahira fell deep into thought, and said, "That's odd, how a cloud is following that caravan." The monk shuddered. He said, "I wonder if..." and hurried to his room.

The novice monk couldn't make anything of Bahira's unfinished words. After watching the monk dash away, he turned back to the caravan. The caravan was resting quietly. There was a mist shimmering like a mirage in the distance. Then he noticed something else.

"There really is a cloud," he said, and was about to go about his business when Bahira stuck his head out of the window and called, "Ahbar, where are you?"

Ahbar ran to the window. Bahira said, "See that caravan? Go there, and invite them all here for a meal."

Ahbar went down the steps and set off. The monk found the cook and told him to prepare a meal.

After the preparations were completed, he waited for Ahbar to return. Ahbar had given the invitation and persuaded those in the caravan to come to the feast. As the preparations were finishing, the guests began to come down the dusty road one by one.

Those in the caravan arrived and sat down to the feast. Instead of eating, the monk Bahira was wandering among the guests. He was looking for someone he could not find.

He asked Abu Talib, "Did everyone in the caravan come to this feast?"

Abu Talib said, "Everyone came, except for a child."

Bahira asked, "Why didn't that child come?"

Abu Talib replied, "We left him with the caravan to guard our belongings."

Bahira said, "Call him too, he should come and eat his meal."

As Bahira served his guests, he became curious about the child to come. Every now and then, he went to the window and looked at the road, and then he returned to his guests. When he saw the shining, beautiful face of Muhammad, he was astonished.

Bahira had many questions. After the feast, he pulled Abu Talib aside and asked, "Who is this child?"

Abu Talib answered in a general way, "He is my son."

Bahira didn't find the answer convincing, "This child cannot be your son."

Abu Talib answered more specifically, "He is my brother's son, but I am his guardian."

"Who is his father?"

"Abdullah."

"Is he alive?"

"No, the child's father died before he was born."

Bahira nodded. This child had all the features he was looking for. But he had to examine him more closely. He pulled the child aside and started to talk with him. He asked him to answer the questions honestly, for the sake of al-Lat and al-Uzza, the "greatest" idols of the Meccan polytheists. The Messenger of Allah made a sour face when he heard the names, and said, "Don't ask me anything in the name of idols. I don't hate anything more than I hate them."

"All right," said Bahira. "In that case, answer honestly in the name of Allah."

"I shall honestly answer what you ask."

After talking for awhile, Bahira understood this child would be the awaited last Messenger, the Seal of the Prophets. But he had to look for one last proof. Then he saw the seal of Prophethood on his back.

It was a dark mole the size of a pigeon egg, between his shoulder blades, described in the books as the mark of the last Prophet. The monk Bahira had no doubts.

Bahira pulled aside Abu Talib and warned, "Take your nephew back to your homeland. He is the awaited last Prophet. If some of the jealous Jews see him, they could harm him." Abu Talib was worried. To prevent any harm from coming to his nephew, he sold his goods there, and returned to Mecca without delay.

Marriage

"They're coming, the caravan is coming!" yelled a young man, spreading the word through Mecca.

At once, the streets turned into a festival. The trade caravan that had gone to Damascus weeks before had finally returned.

Khadija bint Khuwaylid was at home, chatting with her neighbors. One of the women pointed to the sky, to a cloud that seemed to be following the caravan Khadija sent to Damascus for trade. A cloud was shadowing the caravan, seeming to shade it from the sun. There was something different about this caravan.

Later on, Khadija went to her cousin, Waraqa ibn Nawfal. Waraqa was a wise man, learned of the Holy Scriptures. Khadija told him what she had seen and heard about the twenty-five-year-old Muhammad, called al-Amin—the Trustworthy. Not hiding his amazement, Waraqa said, "If what you are saying is true, there is no doubt that this man is a Prophet. I knew that this nation would have a Prophet. That time is exactly now."

Khadija had known of Muhammad the Trustworthy since his childhood. She had put him in charge of her trade caravan. So she had got to know him better. Indeed, she had given the best of her servants, Maysara, to accompany Muhammad the Trustworthy during the entire journey, cautioning him to report back to her everything that he witnessed without skipping a single detail.

Upon their return, Maysara reported all the signs of the awaited Prophet to Khadija, giving every detail of all that he had experienced on the journey. Thereupon, Khadija, a widow who had not thought of marriage for so long, have now made up her mind to marry Muhammad as she could not think of any way to get closer to him other than marriage. She sent her friend, Nafisa, as a messenger.

Nafisa went to him. "O Muhammad, what withholds you from marrying?" she asked.

He was living with his uncle. He did not have the means to get married.

"I have no money. How could I possibly get married?" he replied.

"If the cost of marriage was covered and there was someone suitable for you, would you accept it?"

"Who is it you are talking about?"

"Khadija."

Startled and pleased, he asked, "How could something like that happen?"

"Leave that to me," Nafisa said, smiling.

"In that case, I shall do as you tell me."

Without losing any time, Nafisa gave the good news to Khadija. There was great joy in the house. Preparations were completed quickly. Guests came one by one to Khadija's house. Tables were set for the guests, and meals were served. Towards the end of the wedding feast, the elders made speeches. Waraqa was the last to stand.

"O people of Quraysh! Witness that I marry my uncle Khuwaylid's daughter, Khadija, to Abdullah's son, Muhammad."

That evening was the wedding ceremony for Muhammad and Khadija. After that day, the young man moved out of his uncle Abu Talib's house and into Khadija's house.

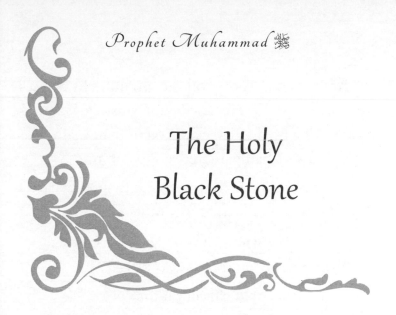

Prophet Muhammad ﷺ

The Holy Black Stone

hose who were rebuilding the Ka'ba, which was about to collapse, were tired. One of them came out of the shade and looked at the rising wall. Rebuilding had gone quickly, and the building had been strengthened. In the quiet, a loud sound came from the back. Two men were yelling in a rage.

The other workers had stood up, and came to see the fight. Two men from different tribes were fighting each other. Hudhayfa, the eldest of them all, came into the middle of the crowd that had gathered.

He asked, "What's happening? What is this fight about?"

35

Amir tried to get up off the ground. His clothes were torn, and he was covered in dust. As soon as he stood, he tried to attack the other man again. But the crowd that had gathered stopped him.

Amir screamed, "He wanted to put Hajaru'l Aswad—the holy Black Stone, in its place."

At these words, everybody spoke at once.

"No way, we will put it into place!"

"No, our people will put it into place!"

The tribes started to quarrel amongst themselves. Every man wanted the honor of placing the Black Stone that had been sent from Paradise. Doing so would gain dignity and status for his tribe.

The argument became so heated that the men were about to kill each other. A riot had begun. Just when the yelling came to a boiling point, Hudhayfa spoke in a thunderous voice, "Stop this! I'm telling you to stop."

The old man's grave voice was obeyed. Every man had stepped back, waiting to hear what he would say. But their tempers were frayed. They were ready to fight at the slightest movement.

Abu Umayya came forward and spoke in a calming way, "I know. Every tribe wants to put this stone in its place. We can't solve this issue among ourselves." He looked around, and thought quickly. "Let's make the first person to enter from the Shayba gate the judge. We shall do whatever he tells us," he said.

No one objected. Everybody was watching the gate to see who would come to arbitrate. The heat had increased, and the wait was growing longer. Who would come? Curious stares were locked on the street. Someone walked through the gate. At once, they knew who it was by his stride, and someone shouted in joy: "It is he, Muhammad!"

"The Trustworthy is coming!"

Amir jumped to his feet and said: "By Allah, we accept whatever he decides on."

Muhammad, peace and blessings be upon him, was an honest, virtuous man who had gained everyone's trust. He could solve this tribal dispute.

They told him about the situation. Then they waited to see what he would do.

He said, "Bring me a cloth." Taking it, he spread it on the ground.

Everyone was now wondering what the cloth was for. Muhammad the Trustworthy placed the holy Black Stone in the middle of the cloth, and said: "One man from each tribe shall hold a corner of the cloth."

With the cloth, they carried the stone to its place and lifted it up all together, bringing honor to every tribe. When the stone came to where it was to be placed, Muhammad, peace and blessings be upon him, took the stone and put it in place. His quick thinking had prevented a riot among the people, and allowed the rebuilding to continue.

Loneliness

any years went by happily in his marriage with Khadija. Muhammad, peace and blessings be upon him, had reached the age of thirty-eight. In those years, he often went away from the city and took walks alone in the valleys and caves that surrounded Mecca. One day, he heard a voice: "Peace be upon you, O Messenger of Allah!"

He immediately turned to see who greeted him. He could see no one and nothing, except a dried-up tree. He carried on a little further. Then a stone on the ground greeted him. Many similar events had been happening lately. He didn't know what was meant by the salutations of various objects or the lights that flashed. His condition went on for a year. At the age of thirty-nine, he started having special, true dreams. Premonitions of things to come would be shown to him in a half-awake, half-asleep state. The dreams that he saw by night were, one by one, coming true by day.

He worried about all these strange, but wonderful things happening to him. Allah Almighty was indeed preparing him for Prophethood. He preferred loneliness to company, and he wandered away from people. He went to quiet, tranquil places and engaged in reflection and devotion.

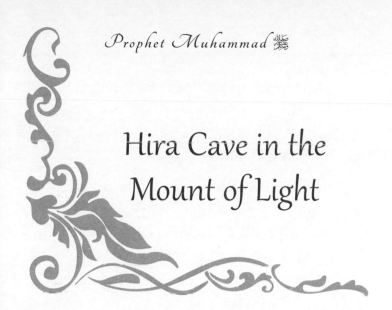

Hira Cave in the Mount of Light

Two men were slowly walking in the desert very early in the morning, and the stars were still shining. It was cool.

The sun hadn't risen but there was a different light brightening the horizon. Two trails of footprints were being left in the desert, and then the wind was blowing them away. With food in his hand, Hasan approached his friend.

He asked, "Will we go on further?"

Thabit, who was tall, looked behind and around them. Then he looked at the Mount of Light.

He finally answered, "We can't return without finding him."

Hasan pointed at the mountain-top cave of Hira. "Could he be in that cave?"

Thabit nodded. "Most likely," he answered.

A blast of wind raised a cloud of sand. They were shocked for a moment, and covered by dust. Hasan grew a little afraid.

"Couldn't we go back? We're very tired. We could take the food later."

As the cloud of sand swirled down, they walked faster. Thabit tugged his friend's hand.

"We made a promise to Khadija. We have to deliver the food."

Thabit started to climb the mountainside, where there was no grass or dried-up tree. The wind had stopped, it was calm now. While they climbed towards the mountainside, it was still early morning with the full moon risen above the desert. They could see around much better on the mountainside. The two young men continued talking.

"I haven't seen him in Mecca for a week," said Thabit.

"That's true. He's staying away from people."

"I wonder why?"

"Why else? There's no justice left, the strong are oppressing the weak. Everybody is tricking each other in trade. How can you not feel bad about these conditions?"

Hasan stopped short, and looked at his friend's face. "But there is someone everybody can trust!"

Thabit looked at him questioningly. With a sweet sigh, gesturing to the cave, Hasan said, "Muhammad the Trustworthy."

"You're right," Thabit replied. "Now, we're almost there. Let's deliver the food and return."

After giving Muhammad the Trustworthy the water and food, the two young men returned to Mecca.

He stayed in the cave and prayed to Allah until all the food was gone. Then he came out of the cave. The heat had increased, and the desert was boiling hot.

He was alone until after he had entered the streets of Mecca. He went straight to the Ka'ba. Some people were worshipping idols, some were

43

chatting, and some were leaning on a wall sleeping. The Messenger of Allah walked past them and performed *tawaf*, circling the Ka'ba. Then he returned home.

Khadija met him at the door and welcomed him inside. She was very happy about his return. For a long time, her husband had been withdrawing from society, spending most of his time in deep reflection and devotion to his Lord.

Khadija, may Allah be pleased with her, was helping him as much as she could, sending him water and food. But when he didn't come back for many days, she worried and sent someone to check on him.

He told Khadija about the things he saw and heard. He was seeing flashes and hearing salutations of creation when he was alone. He was afraid of these visions and sounds.

"I am afraid of becoming a soothsayer! I swear to Allah, I don't hate anything more than I hate idols and soothsayers."

Khadija replied, "Allah will never forsake you and will not allow anything bad to happen to you, because you always protect what is entrusted to you, you do good to your relatives, and you tell the truth in all your words."

In the following days, he went again to the cave. Another cloudless night had begun. There was nobody around. Stars in the sky were brighter than ever, and so close to the ground that you would think they were going to fall. In the late hours of the night, the Messenger of Allah fell asleep.

Near dawn, a pleasant breeze started to blow. The cave was filled with beautiful scents. The horizon started to turn red, and the sun was rising. The dark cave filled with light suddenly. Gabriel, the archangel of Revelation, had come to the cave in the form of a handsome man. He appeared with a dazzling brightness.

Among those lovely smells, with a loud voice, Archangel Gabriel said: "Read!"

Muhammad, peace and blessings be upon him, said: "I do not know how to read!"

Archangel Gabriel embraced and squeezed him. He nearly choked him. The Angel of Revelation again said: "Read!"

"I do not know how to read, tell me what I should read," he replied.

Archangel Gabriel embraced and squeezed our Prophet for the third time and conveyed the first Revelation (which means): *"Read in and with the Name of your Lord Who has created! Created the human from a clot clinging (to the wall of the womb). Read, and your Lord is the All-Munificent, who has taught by the pen, taught (human) by the pen—taught human what he knew not."*

The blessed Prophet repeated the verses word for word. The verses were written in the Messenger's tongue and heart. Archangel Gabriel then disappeared suddenly.

Muhammad, peace and blessings be upon him, came out of the cave terrified and exhilarated. Without losing time, he set off for Mecca. Allah had made him a Prophet. He came home, shivering, and said: "O Khadija, cover me," and got into bed. Khadija had waited curiously for him to come home. Even though she saw the difference in the noble Prophet's face, she didn't ask him anything. She waited until his fear and shivering had subsided.

After a while, the blessed Prophet woke up. He told his beloved wife exactly what had happened and said: "I am afraid, O Khadija! I am afraid of being harmed."

Khadija listened to it all in silence. She supported him and when he was finished she said, "Be constant! I swear by Allah that I hope that you are the Prophet of this nation."

Ali ibn Abi Talib

rchangel Gabriel had taught the Messenger of Allah how to perform *wudu*, washing parts of the body in preparation for *Salah*, the Prescribed Prayers. The noble Prophet taught these things to his beloved wife, who had become the first Muslim. They were praying at home together. Ali ibn Abi Talib, who was only a child, saw them when he entered the room. He watched them in curiosity. As soon as the Prayers were finished, he asked, "What is this?"

The beloved Prophet patted Ali's head and embraced him. With a smile, he said, "We prayed."

Ali ibn Abi Talib was hearing this word for the first time.

"Well, what is it?"

"It is worshiping Allah!"

"What is worshiping?"

"It is servitude to Allah, Who has created the universe. We bowed to Him, and did prostration to Him. We did our servitude, O Ali." The Messenger of Allah then asked Ali to be with them, too.

But Ali's questions hadn't finished yet.

"What does that mean?"

"Become a Muslim. I am inviting you to the religion of the one and only Allah. Would you accept my invitation, O Ali?"

His uncle's son Ali's big black eyes shone, and he said, "This is something I have never heard of before. I can't decide without consulting my father."

But the noble Prophet was not openly preaching Islam in those days. So he warned, "O Ali! If you do what I tell you, do it! But, if you aren't going to do it, keep it secret. Don't tell anybody about it (except your father)."

Ali ibn Abi Talib promised he wouldn't tell anyone else about this secret, and then he left. He passed the night thinking about it. As the sun was rising, he felt better. He had made his decision. He came to the Messenger of Allah and said, "What did you offer me yesterday?"

"You will witness that there is no deity but Allah, and that He has no partner. Forsake the al-Lat and al-Uzza idols. Refrain from associating any partners to Allah."

Then, he asked Ali, may Allah be pleased with him, "Did you consult your father?"

Young Ali replied, "Allah didn't ask my father when He was creating me, so why should I consult my father to worship Him?"

Then he declared the oneness and absolute unity of Allah, accepted Muhammad as His Messenger, and thereby became one of the first Muslims, and one of the first who prayed.

Abu Bakr

a wise old man was walking back and forth in his house. He was so excited that his heart was pounding, and his face was flushed. He was holding his chin, thinking, and asking questions to the blessed guest who had come to his house. The answers he got exhilarated him even more.

Abu Bakr had finished his meal and was having a cold drink. He couldn't understand why the wise man was hovering around him, and cherishing him.

Aware of the signs of the awaited Prophet and his closest Companion, the wise old man turned to

Abu Bakr and said, "There's one thing left that I want to know."

"What is it?"

The old man suddenly squatted and said, "Show me your belly."

Shocked, Abu Bakr didn't know how to reply. After thinking for a while, he responded, "Not unless you tell me why you want this."

The wise old man looked into Abu Bakr's eyes. He thought he had arrived at the moment he had been waiting on for years.

"Holy Books give tidings of a Prophet to come. This Prophet will appear in Mecca. I found out that a young person and a mature person will support him. You might be that mature person. You are white-skinned and slim. There should be a mole on your belly. Now you know. Come on, show me your belly."

Upon this, Abu Bakr rose and opened his robe. When the wise old man saw the mole on his belly, he shrieked in joy. "You are the person I was talking about. You will be his supporter."

Abu Bakr, who had always refrained from the ignorance and mischief of Jahiliyya, the Age of Ignorance, was pleased by the good news. He had a long conversation with the wise old man. He asked about the Messenger of Allah who was to come. The information he received showed him who the noble Prophet was.

A few days later, the caravan that Abu Bakr was in, set off from Yemen towards Mecca.

The merchants in the caravan were tired from travelling for weeks. They were scorched by the dry air and the hot sun of the desert. When Mecca appeared in the distance, they thought of their hardship coming to an end, drinking cold water, and relaxing. They were pleased about doing profitable trade.

Abu Bakr had different thoughts. He was still thinking of the words of the wise old man. He had been given good tidings of a Prophet to come, and that he would be his closest supporter.

Who could that Prophet be?

When Abu Bakr returned home, Shayba, Abu Jahl, and other friends came to visit him. He asked them, "Did anything important happen while I was away?"

"What didn't happen! Abu Talib's orphan says that he is a Prophet. We waited for you to return. Go and tell him whatever you will. You are his closest friend. If it wasn't for you we would have dealt with him by now."

After sending off his guests appropriately, without losing time, Abu Bakr went to the noble Prophet's house and knocked on the door. "O Muhammad! Is the news I hear about you true?" he asked.

The noble Prophet, peace and blessings be upon him, smiled and asked, "O Abu Bakr, what news about me have you heard?"

"You call to believe in the Oneness and absolute Unity of Allah, and say that you are the Messenger of Allah."

"Yes, O Abu Bakr. I am a Prophet sent to you and all humankind. I am inviting people to the One and Only Allah. You should believe too," he said.

Abu Bakr knew well about his honesty, trustworthiness, and high morals. However, he had a concern. "What is your proof?" he asked.

The Messenger of Allah replied, smiling, "The wise old man you came across in Yemen." When he said what the wise old man had said, Abu Bakr believed wholeheartedly.

"By Allah, I never encountered a lie in you. You are worthy of being sent as a Prophet." Abu Bakr, may Allah be pleased with him, embraced Islam there and then.

Abu Bakr becoming a Muslim pleased our Prophet greatly. Abu Bakr, who was intelligent and honest, caused many of his close friends to be Muslims, too.

Slave

*I*t was midday. The market was very crowded. Sellers were yelling, and customers were trying to buy the best goods.

One of the fabric merchants got up on something high. Just when he was about to call out, a crowd of kids entered the marketplace. The child leading the group was holding a rope. The rope was tied to the neck of the slave being mocked and abused.

The children had pushed into the crowd loudly. They were having fun in tormenting the black slave. The slave was Bilal al-Habashi, may Allah be pleased with him. He crossed the marketplace from one end to the other, not caring what was done to him.

"Look at his situation. He entered Muhammad's religion."

"He asked for it."

"He deserves it."

Sometimes they even threw dust and stones at him.

Bilal al-Habashi was being punished by his owner because he said, "Ahad" (Allah is The Unique One). Sometimes he was left hungry and thirsty for hours, and sometimes he was taken around the marketplace with a rope around his neck. No matter what Bilal's owner, Umayya ibn Halaf, did, he failed to make him renounce his faith.

Finally he laid him on hot sand, and tormented him. He placed a little idol icon on Bilal's face and screamed, "Accept al-Lat and al-Uzza!"

Bilal, who could hardly open his eyes, said only, "There is one Allah! There is one Allah!"

Umayya stood up angrily. He said, "Bring that rock." His helpers started to drag a heavy rock.

Umayya asked Bilal one last time to renounce his faith. There was no change in Bilal's answer. He said, "Put the rock on top of him."

His men did as Umayya told them. Bilal was nearly crushed by the weight of the rock. He was breathing heavily. At that moment, Abu Bakr passed by. When he saw what was happening, he couldn't stand it. He wanted to save Bilal al-Habashi. Umayya called out to Abu Bakr, "You ruined him. If you want to save him, you'll have to buy him."

Abu Bakr said, "I have a slave of your religion. He is stronger than Bilal. I'll give him to you in exchange for Bilal. Would you accept it?"

Umayya was happy about the bargain. But he grinned and said, "I accept it. But only if you give me the slave's wife and daughter, too."

Abu Bakr said, "All right."

Umayya started to make trouble. "No deal, unless you give me two hundred dinars as well."

Abu Bakr was displeased by Umayya's increasing requests. Umayya said, "That is all I will ask for."

So Abu Bakr gave him two hundred dinars, and the other slaves, and bought Bilal al-Habashi.

After saving Bilal from the hands of Umayya, Abu Bakr went to the noble Prophet. Allah's Messenger, peace and blessings be upon him, was very pleased. He said to Abu Bakr: "O Abu Bakr! Will you have rights over him?"

Abu Bakr said, "No, O Allah's Messenger. I liberated him."

After his liberation, Bilal al-Habashi never left the noble Prophet's side. He was a muezzin, and for many years he called Muslims to the Daily Prayers.

Invitation

$\mathcal{A}$ new day was beginning in Mecca. Safiyya, the noble Prophet's aunt, was rather worried.

She got dressed and went out. The market had opened and it became crowded. Poets were walking in the streets reading poems. Some people were bringing the idols they made to the Ka'ba, and others were cleaning the idols.

As Safiyya walked quickly, she was wondering why Prophet Muhammad, peace and blessings be upon him, had not left his house for a long time. What if something had happened to him, or what if he was ill?

She and his other aunts reached the noble
Prophet's house. The blessed Prophet said, "I am
not ill and have no complaint. But Allah ordered
me to warn my close relatives about the torment to
come. I want to gather the sons and daughters of
Abdul Muttalib, and invite them to belief in Allah."

His aunts said he should invite all his relatives,
except Abu Lahab. Then they left.

Allah the Almighty had ordered the Messenger
of Allah to invite others to Islam. So the noble
Prophet called Ali ibn Abi Talib, and said, "Make a
meat dish enough for one person. And fill one container with milk. Then gather the sons and daughters of Abdul Muttalib. I am going to talk with
them, and tell them what I am ordered to do."

The guests started to come to the house of the
Messenger of Allah. They waited curiously to see
what would happen. When they saw a meat dish for
only one person and a single container of milk, they
were surprised and displeased. They talked among
themselves in a disparaging manner.

Abu Lahab murmured, "Look! Are we all going
to eat from a single plate of food? This isn't even
enough for me."

Someone else laughed and said, "And he claims to be a Prophet." The Messenger of Allah was offended, but he didn't reply. He said only, "Bismillah" (in the Name of Allah), and cut up the meat.

Those who had come started to eat. As they ate, they were surprised. Even though they were eating and drinking as much as they liked, neither the meat nor the milk was gone. They were amazed by the miracle. Some of them softened, but Abu Lahab mocked, "I have never seen such magic." He insulted the noble Prophet.

The Messenger of Allah told them about the One and Only Allah and His glorious religion. Then he asked those who were there, "Who will help me?" His relatives, who had eaten and drunk to their hearts' content, kept silent. They bowed their heads.

Even though nobody would say a word, Ali ibn Abi Talib stood up. The blessed Prophet said, "Sit down." He repeated the same question three times. Every time Ali stood and replied, "O Messenger of Allah, I will help you."

The others sneered at the twelve-year-old boy. "He's only a small child. What use will his help be?" Not taking the noble Prophet's invitation seriously, they left the house.

His relatives had walked out on him, but Muhammad, peace and blessings be upon him, continued to tell people about Islam in the following days.

I Will not Give Up

The pilgrim population had grown in Mecca. The number of people shopping had increased. There was a boost in the number of caravans coming lately. Abu Sufyan, a leading man of Mecca, walked down the streets. His servant was right behind him, following him with a fan.

He walked past the sellers and turned into a side street. He stopped in front of a large white house. The servant waiting at the entrance welcomed him with respect.

When he entered the big room, he saw that Abu Jahl was very angry. Abu Jahl took a bunch of grapes from a plate, handed it to Abu Sufyan, and said,

"Welcome, Abu Sufyan. We were waiting for you to come."

Abu Sufyan did not know what was going on. He was silent, expecting an explanation.

The host, Walid, stood up. Everybody quieted down, watching him.

"The Hajj season is near. Caravans have started to arrive already. They will have questions about Muhammad." He made a wry face, and looked at those in the room. He said in a strong voice, "What will you tell them?"

The question had brought an angry scowl to all their faces. Abu Jahl grinned and said, "We will say he is a magician or a soothsayer. Thus, they won't believe him."

The host sat on a cushion and laughed. He said, thoughtfully, "Everybody will say different things. You will contradict each other and be at odds."

"True," said Abu Lahab. "We should agree and say the same thing."

Walid felt this conversation wasn't going to come to a satisfactory conclusion. He said, "It will be understood that your words are groundless." He was silent for awhile. Then he raised his head, and recommended that they call him a magician.

The servants brought cold drinks. Abu Jahl had a bright idea, and said, "Let's visit his uncle." Abu Lahab seconded him, "They are speaking ill of the idols again. They are talking about their religion openly. We have to stop this."

The others shared his thoughts. After finishing their meal, they walked out into the street as a crowd. A little later, they knocked on the door of Abu Talib.

"O Abu Talib, your nephew has gone too far. He is speaking out against our idols. He is disparaging our ancestors' religion. Your nephew should stop what he is doing. He shouldn't discredit our grandfathers. He shouldn't insult our idols. Tell him to give up on this mission of his. If he wants to be a leader, we shall make him our leader. If he wants to be rich, we will make him rich. We will give him our riches. We will marry him to the most beautiful girls in Mecca. As long as he gives up his mission."

They silently stared at each other for awhile, and then said: "Either he will give up doing these things, or we will fight until one of us is annihilated."

These last words hurt Abu Talib deeply. He had protected his nephew until now, but the polytheists were talking about a war. Abu Talib didn't want to fall out with his tribe, and he didn't want to be abandoned by them. But he couldn't find it in his heart to hand over his nephew to them, either.

He said, "I shall talk to my nephew Muhammad." He sent someone for the noble Prophet. When the Messenger of Allah arrived, Abu Talib faced him and said, "O my brother's son! The dignitaries of my tribe came to me."

And he explained that he couldn't put up with all these difficulties. He asked him not to talk about the idols, and cautioned him not to interfere with their religion. Then he passed on the polytheists' threat. Abu Talib was sad, and with a hoarse voice he said, "Please, have pity on me and yourself. Don't put us both under loads that we can't carry."

The Messenger of Allah, peace and blessings be upon him, was very troubled by these words. He thought his uncle would not be able to help or support him anymore. But his course was set by a higher authority. "O uncle, I swear by Allah, if they were to put the sun in my right hand and the moon in my left hand, I still will not give up my mission." The noble Prophet's eyes filled with tears. Then he stood up and walked toward the door.

In distress, Abu Talib cried out to his nephew, "Come back, O son of my brother! O my nephew, do what you wish, say what you wish. This uncle of yours will always protect you. And he will never leave you alone." And he hugged him.

Then he stepped out of the room. The polytheists were waiting in anticipation. When Abu Talib relayed the blessed Prophet's answer, they all made a sour face. Then they threatened him, "We are not responsible for what will happen to your nephew." They left his house in anger.

Out on the street, Abu Jahl angrily knocked over his own servant. All the polytheists deliberated what they were going to do, since they had not gotten what they wanted.

The Moon Is Split

The Messenger of Allah, peace and blessings be upon him, was sitting with a few of his Companions, having a conversation. From those bright lips, words were flowing like the waterfalls of paradise, warming their hearts. They wanted time to stop; they couldn't bear for anything to interrupt these talks.

Just then, a group of men from the Quraysh showed up. Abu Jahl was among them. It was obvious that they weren't there to chat. One of them came forward and said to the noble Prophet, "Since you say that you are a prophet, show us a miracle so we can believe. Split the moon in half. Can you do that?"

In the face of this offer, the noble Prophet calmly looked at them one by one. Then he turned his eyes to the moon. There wasn't a cloud in the sky. Stars had slowly started to appear. The moon was in its most beautiful state, hanging among the stars like a round tray.

The blessed Prophet asked them, "If I do as you wish, will you believe?"

Without hesitation, the people of the Quraysh replied, "Of course we will! As long as you show us this miracle."

The Messenger of Allah, peace and blessings be upon him, prayed to Allah first. Then he stood up. He raised his index finger and pointed to the moon. He moved his finger downward in a straight line, as if he was cutting something.

Those who were there were amazed. Both the polytheists and the noble Prophet's Companions were astonished. They were witnessing a miracle right before their eyes.

The moon had split in two. One half was above Mount Abu Qubays, and the other half was above Mount Quayqian. There was quite a distance between them.

The Messenger of Allah turned to his Companions and said, "Be witnesses! Be witnesses!"

Abu Jahl rubbed his eyes and looked again. And again. For a moment, he didn't know what to say or do. When he pulled himself together, he forgot his promise. "The magic of Abu Talib's orphan affected the heavens too," he said.

When he heard these words, the noble Prophet was very unhappy. Then, in the sky, the pieces of the moon started to move toward each other. Finally they came together, as it used to be, as if it had never been split.

One of the polytheists screamed: "He cast a spell over us! Let's see if people coming to Mecca have seen this too. If they haven't seen it, Muhammad has definitely cast a spell on us. Muhammad couldn't have cast a spell over all people!"

A curious wait started. After some time, a caravan came into town. The polytheists ran toward it with great excitement. But as they got closer to it, they saw by their faces that they were in awe, too. It was clear that this miracle had been seen by others. The polytheists couldn't find anything new to say. They kept saying: "This is clearly magic!"

Soon after, Allah the Almighty announced this miracle to everyone by Revelation (which means): *"The Last Hour has drawn near, and the moon has split. Whenever they see a miracle, they turn from it in aversion and say: 'This is sorcery like many others, one after the other.'"* (al-Qamar 54:1–2).

A Maggot

ight had fallen on the streets; people in the marketplace had started to go home. A slim woman hidden near the corner of the street looked around.

When she was sure there was nobody around, she pulled her cover over her face. She looked at the street one last time, walked quickly, and leapt into a shop with closed windows. After going inside, she turned around and looked back. She was out of breath.

The old shopkeeper spoke quietly. "Did anyone see you?"

"No," she breathed, shaking her head. The hungry and thirsty woman could barely speak.

"I know," said the shopkeeper, handing her a bundle of goods. "They are going too far. They are doing everything they can to annihilate you."

With fear in her eyes, the woman hung the bundle over her shoulder. She covered them with her clothing. "The boycott is continuing. Our children have started to die of hunger."

"Allah willing, it will end soon."

"I have to leave immediately. The Muslims are waiting for me."

"Be cautious. Don't let anyone see you leaving here, or else they'll destroy my shop."

The shopkeeper believed in Allah secretly. He was helping Muslims who were in hardship secretly, too.

"I know. May Allah be pleased with you," said the woman with sincerity.

The old man's eyes filled with tears. "Come early in the morning tomorrow. I'll prepare food for you."

The woman scanned the streets before leaving, and quietly exited the shop. In the streets of Mecca, she walked furtively. With shaky steps, she feared someone confronting her at every turn. Walking past the Ka'ba, she turned her head to its gate. On the gate, there was a piece of paper. The paper had been put there weeks ago.

When they realized that they couldn't prevent Islam from spreading, the polytheists had united. They decided to boycott Muslims: they weren't going to do business with or sell anything to them, nor allow marriages between the two societies. Those who helped them would be punished, too. They had forced Muslims together in a ghetto outside of Mecca, and they weren't allowing food or drink to pass.

The following day, the now elderly Abu Talib had come into Mecca. Polytheists gave the news immediately to Abu Jahl, who with his friends, was pleased. Perhaps the Muslims were going to retreat after the oppression and cruelty.

The weather was rather cool. Different kinds of fruit lay before the people. Some standing, some sitting, they were listening to Abu Talib, "My brother's son has sent you a message. Allah has sent a maggot to destroy the paper you have hung on the wall of the Ka'ba, on which the boycott decision was written. This maggot has eaten all of the decisions you wrote. The only part left is where Allah's name is written."

Those who were sitting opened their eyes wide, and jumped to their feet as fear overtook them.

Abu Talib continued, "If my nephew is right, end this ill-conduct of yours. But if nothing has happened to the paper, I will hand him over to you. You are free to kill him or leave him alive, as you wish."

A rush began. A large mob of polytheists ran toward the Ka'ba. They pushed aside everyone in their path. There was a single question on their minds. Was what Abu Talib said true? Abu Jahl, who reached the gate of the Ka'ba, was astounded. All could see that the paper had been eaten by a maggot. One took the scrap of paper in his hands. Only Allah's name was left. When they saw this, to prevent any one of them from believing, they said, "This too is magic."

But the boycott against Muslims had been broken. Though some wished to continue oppressing the Muslims, they fell into disagreement with each other. The Muslims were freed of their suffering.

Khadija's wealth had evaporated during the years of the boycott. As her money went, so did her health, and she passed away. Three days before this, Abu Talib had died. So many sad events, one after another, caused the Messenger of Allah to name this time "The Year of Sorrow."

The Ascension

At this low moment, in a life filled with sadness, the Archangel Gabriel came to the Messenger of Allah when he was resting at the place called Hatim, next to the Ka'ba. He put the noble Prophet on a mount named Buraq, and they set off together.

Buraq was a very interesting mount. Its steps were so vast that it could reach the horizon in a single leap. In a short time, they reached Jerusalem. The Messenger of Allah dismounted. All of the Prophets and Messengers of the past were waiting for him there. At the site of Al-Aqsa Mosque, the noble Prophet went straight to the front. He became the imam, the prayer leader, for all the Prophets of Allah. They prayed altogether.

After the Prayer the Messenger of Allah and Archangel Gabriel rose into the sky. Archangel Gabriel stopped when they reached a point called Sidratu'l-Muntaha—the Lote-tree of the furthest limit.

The blessed Prophet continued alone into the heavens. Sometime later, Allah's Messenger came into Our Lord's presence. He talked with Him.

He then toured Paradise with the angels. He saw the inconceivable beauties of Paradise. Houris and angels begged for him to stay. But the blessed Prophet remembered his *ummah*, his people. The five Daily Prayers were set that night. Following the same route, the beloved Prophet returned to Mecca.

In the morning, he went to the Quraysh. He told them he had been to Jerusalem the night before. They were dazed by this, for a journey to Jerusalem took many weeks. One of them said, "This is something unseen. Can you prove that this really happened?"

"I came across a caravan that was coming here. There was a camel at the front of the caravan that was blackish. There were two sacks on it, one white and one black," said the Messenger of Allah.

The polytheists didn't know what to say. The noble Prophet continued, "I saw another caravan. They were sleeping. They had a covered jug. I drank the water in that jug. Then I covered it again."

The people of the Quraysh were listening, breathless, to the blessed Prophet. They were excited. The beloved Prophet said, "I encountered a few men on the way. They were looking for their lost camel. I told them where their camel was. Then I went toward Damascus."

The polytheists thought about his story for awhile. They were hesitant whether to believe. They all knew he had not told a single lie in all his life, not even as a joke. They knew he would never make up a story like this.

One of them stood. Looking around at the others, he said, "Muhammad has not lied before today. But still, let us verify the truth of these words. Let us set off immediately. We shall greet the people that he claimed he saw, and we will ask them about this."

They went to wait for the caravans at the entrance of the city. After some time, one came. The polytheists ran toward the group with great anticipation. They were frozen by the sight they saw close up. They whispered amongst themselves.

"But how can this be? The camel at the front is blackish, exactly as he said!"

"And of the two sacks on the camel, one is white and the other is black..."

"Muhammad told us the truth!"

The polytheists were dumbfounded. They couldn't say a single word. One of them broke the silence, "Let's wait for the other caravan too."

They waited a little longer. Finally a long shadow appeared on the horizon. It was the caravan they were waiting for. They ran to it in curiosity. The people in the caravan felt the strangeness that hovered over the Quraysh. They asked, "What happened? Why are you so excited?"

Panting for breath, the men answered, "Where is your water jug?"

The people of the caravan could not make sense of this question.

"Here it is," said one.

"Did anything odd happen to this jug on the way?"

"Yes, it did."

"What is it?"

"The jug was full of water. And it was covered. We were asleep. When we woke up, there wasn't a single drop of water in it. And the cover was on it exactly as before."

The Quraysh squatted where they were, silent. The people of the caravan were looking at them strangely, trying to understand their odd behavior. But the Quraysh were in no state to talk. Finally, unwillingly, one of them spoke.

"Friends, let us investigate the lost camel. One of us should go and find those men, and ask what happened last night."

One of them jumped on his horse and set off at once. When he returned, his shoulders were stooped. From the look on his face, the people of the Quraysh knew that this, too, was true. The man bowed his head. "I found the owners of the camel. Muhammad has told us the truth."

The Quraysh began to brood. Their stubbornness prevented them from believing. One of them turned to the blessed Prophet and asked, "Come on, tell us. Can you describe Al-Aqsa Mosque to us?"

The noble Prophet did not hesitate. He began to describe what he had seen the night before. As he spoke, the man who asked the question changed color. The others knew from his countenance that the beloved Prophet's words were accurate. The man interrupted, "Well, how many doors does the Al-Aqsa Mosque have?"

The Messenger of Allah was becoming very troubled. Despite all his evidence, these men were very unwilling to believe. At the question he was silent, because he hadn't counted the doors of Al-Aqsa Mosque. But at that moment, a miracle only visible to the noble Prophet occurred. Allah the Almighty brought Al-Aqsa Mosque, in all its beauty, before his eyes. He counted the doors and told the man. And he didn't stop there. He began to describe, in great detail, the features of Al-Aqsa Mosque that even they didn't know. The polytheists gave up saying, "All right, all right. Everything you said is perfectly true."

But they still didn't become Muslims. Instead, they pondered how they could use this story against the Muslims. A few of them found the noble Prophet's closest friend, Abu Bakr.

They asked, "Did you hear about it? Your friend says that he went to Al-Aqsa Mosque last night. He supposedly prayed there and came back."

Abu Bakr was not shocked at all. He asked, calmly, "Did he tell you of it?" The polytheists laughed and nodded, "Yes, he said it. It's amazing, isn't it?"

"No, if he said it, I swear by Allah he is telling the truth. Why are you surprised? I believe revelations are coming from the heavens to the noble Prophet; why should I not believe this?"

The polytheists gaped in astonishment. They didn't know what to say. So they turned around and went back.

With the miracle of the Night Journey and Ascension, Allah the Almighty had consoled the beloved Prophet, who had lost two of the people he loved the most. Allah was simply saying, "O Muhammad, don't be sad! I am always with you."

Prophet Muhammad ﷺ

Migration

*I*t was midday. It was a normal day in Mecca. Many Muslims, one by one, had migrated to Medina due to the unbearable persecutions in their hometown. Hearing of the migration, the polytheists had stepped up their oppression and torture of the remaining Muslims. Thus everyone had gone to Medina except the noble Prophet, Abu Bakr, Ali ibn Abi Talib, and a few other Muslims.

Two people entered the street and went straight to the bakery. The smell of fresh bread wafted through the bazaar, on a slight breeze carrying the scent into the streets. It was midday and some people realized they were hungry.

The street behind the bazaar was empty. A little while later, the noble Prophet walked by. It was something he didn't normally do. He was visiting in the midday heat, though normally he visited in the cool of the morning or toward evening. But today, an important issue took him out of his house in the midday heat.

He knocked on Abu Bakr's door. "The Messenger of Allah has come," they said.

Abu Bakr stood up, startled by the noble Prophet coming at an unexpected time.

"I swear by Allah, the Messenger of Allah would never come at this time of the day. He definitely has something important to say," he thought, and welcomed the blessed Prophet.

"O Messenger of Allah, welcome! What's the news?"

The blessed Prophet told him that Allah the Almighty had given him permission for migration. Upon hearing this, Abu Bakr grew excited. His mind was burning with a question and he wondered what the answer was.

"Am I going with you?" he asked.

When the noble Prophet said yes, Abu Bakr started to cry in sheer joy.

They sat and planned the journey together. They made an agreement with Abdullah ibn Urayqit to guide them. The guide was to come to the meeting point three nights later with two camels. After completing the preparations, the noble Prophet returned home.

The night the beloved Prophet was going to depart, he called Ali ibn Abi Talib and said, "Sleep in my bed tonight. And pull this cover over you. No harm will come to you from them."

Ali ibn Abi Talib lay in the noble Prophet's bed that night. Toward the morning, the Messenger of Allah recited Ya-Sin, a chapter of the Qur'an, and unseen, walked through the polytheists that had come to kill him.

The morning was cool, and there was no one in the streets. The stars were shining bright in the sky. The day was near. Two men took a road that passed through the streets, without being seen by anyone, and reached the desert. Abu Bakr was anxious. He was looking around, worried that someone could be following them. He scanned the horizon, worried that someone was waiting for them. Sometimes he walked behind the noble Prophet, sometimes he walked ahead of the Messenger of Allah just to protect him from any possible dangers.

The noble Prophet saw Abu Bakr's actions and asked, "O Abu Bakr! Why are you sometimes walking in front of me and sometimes behind me?"

"As I remember that you are being searched for, I walk behind you, and as soon as I recall that they are watching out for you, I walk in front of you," he answered.

"O Abu Bakr! Do you want a disaster that is coming to me, to come to you instead?"

"Yes! I swear to Allah who sent you with the true religion that I prefer a disaster that is coming to befall on me." His sincerity expressed how much he loved the blessed Prophet.

After traveling for about an hour, they reached Mount Thawr. When they reached the mouth of the cave on the mountainside, Abu Bakr went in first and cleaned it out. Then he blocked the holes with scraps of cloth he ripped from his robes. But a small hole remained. When he was finished, he invited the blessed Prophet in.

The Messenger of Allah put his head on Abu Bakr's knee and quickly fell asleep. Meanwhile Abu Bakr had blocked the open hole with one of his heels. A while later, he felt a tremendous pain in his heel. A snake had bitten him. He endured the pain so the noble Prophet wouldn't wake up. But it was so painful that he couldn't stop tears from falling. These tears dropped onto the blessed Prophet's cheek. Our beloved Prophet opened his eyes and asked, "What happened, O Abu Bakr?"

"O Messenger of Allah, a snake bit me. But it's not important."

The noble Prophet rubbed his saliva on the snakebite, and the pain was gone instantly. The two friends continued to wait in the small cave.

Pigeon and Spider

The polytheists had a grudge. They were searching for the noble Prophet and Abu Bakr in the desert. The leading tracker was looking at the ground, searching for a trace, and then showing the way. Following their trail, they had come to Mount Thawr.

Abu Jahl got off his horse and approached the tracker. "Are you sure they're here?" he asked. The tracker was old and experienced. "I'm sure. The traces come this far and stop," he replied.

Suraqa, who was at the back of the group, squinted. He looked from the mountainside to the vast desert stretching before them. "Let's search then."

The tracks came to the mountainside and stopped. The polytheists were slowly getting closer to the cave. Abu Bakr was very anxious and troubled. The noble Prophet said, "Don't worry. Allah is with us."

The tracker pointed to the cave. "There, there is a trace on that rock. I swear to Allah they haven't gone further than this cave."

The polytheists got off their horses and pulled out their swords.

"You haven't been mistaken yet, have you?" they asked.

The old tracker was certain. "I have never been mistaken," he replied.

One of them approached the cave. He looked around a bit and came back to the others. Abu Jahl asked, "What happened, why didn't you look in the cave?"

"There's no need to," he said, and looked at the tracker with doubtful eyes. "They can't have gone in there."

Abu Jahl was a little angry. "Why not?" he demanded.

"Because there is a cobweb at the entrance of the cave."

Abu Jahl and those with him went to the mouth of the cave.

The young tracker said, "A pigeon has made a nest here too. If there were anyone in the cave, the pigeon wouldn't be here."

Abu Jahl was losing his temper. He looked at the old tracker with anger. He was looking for someone to blame.

One of them put his hand on the stone of the cave and said, "Let's go into the cave and have a look."

Umayya pulled back his arm in a rage. "Don't you have any sense? Look at that web. This web must have been spun before Muhammad was born." He started stomping down the mountainside. He called back, "If we hurry, we might catch up with them at the water wells."

Abu Jahl was dumbfounded. They mounted their horses and turned away.

Inside the cave, Abu Bakr was deeply anxious. Lifting his head slightly, he could see the feet of the polytheists. "O, Allah's Prophet. If one of them bends over and looks, they will see us."

The noble Prophet answered, "Be quiet O Abu Bakr! We are two and Allah is the third."

As the polytheists rode away, the spider continued to spin its web, and the pigeon waited for its eggs to hatch. Allah the Almighty had protected the blessed Prophet and Abu Bakr from the polytheists by means of a pigeon and a spider.

Medina

They had been waiting for the guest to come from the desert since the morning, and they were tired. And it was rather hot. There was nobody under the palm trees. Everybody had gone home.

Those who were waiting had given up watching, when one of them started to shout, "There they are! They're coming."

Far away, in the mirages and mists of the desert, a few people dressed in white could be seen.

Upon this call, everybody rejoiced. The people of Medina went out to welcome the noble Prophet, despite the burning sun.

Those who went out to welcome him found the Messenger of Allah resting under a palm tree. There was a sense of joy in Medina, as they rejoined the blessed guests they had been waiting on for days.

The noble Prophet spent the night in the village of Quba near Medina. A mosque was built in Quba. After staying for about ten days, Allah's Messenger continued on to Medina.

When the blessed guest entered the city, Medina was shaking with joy. Men, women, and children were on their rooftops, calling out, "O Muhammad, O Allah's Messenger!"

Some of them had a tambourine in their hands to celebrate the arrival of the blessed Prophet.

They sang: "The full moon is shining on us from the area of gardens. We must offer thanks (to Allah) so long as anyone prays before Allah."

Among this fanfare, the beloved Prophet continued on his camel. Someone approached his camel and ambitiously said, "O Allah's Messenger, be our guest."

Many people wanted to host him in their homes. Allah's Messenger didn't want to hurt anyone's feelings. So he let go of his camel's reins. "Give room to the camel. She has been told where to kneel down."

The crowd moved back. The camel, Qaswa, started to proceed slowly. Everybody followed the camel in curiosity. She knelt down somewhere and started to bellow. After the noble Prophet dismounted his camel, he said, "Allah willing, this is our destination."

Time had passed and it was getting dark. Medinans couldn't leave the noble Prophet in their eagerness to take him into their homes. The Messenger of Allah said, "Tonight I shall stay with the sons of Najjar, who are uncles of my grandfather Abdul Muttalib." And then he added, "Of our relatives, whose house is the closest?"

Abu Ayyub answered, "It is mine, O Prophet of Allah. If you allow me, I shall carry your belongings on the camel." The other people present didn't want to settle for this. The noble Prophet said, "A person should be next to their mount and belongings." It was obvious where he was going to pass the night.

Among demonstrations of affection, the blessed Prophet went to Abu Ayyub al-Ansari's house.

Trade Caravan

*I*t was the second year of the Migration. Meccan polytheists had prepared a trade caravan of more than one thousand camels. They were taking the confiscated goods to Damascus to sell.

With the money they made, they planned to establish an army to annihilate the Muslims. This was the real reason for the caravan. Forty soldiers protected the caravan. Worst of all, most of the goods the caravan was carrying had belonged to the Muslims who migrated.

Abu Sufyan led the caravan, and when it returned from Damascus, the noble Prophet was informed of the sinister motive of the polytheists.

So the Muslims prepared an army, to intercept the caravan at Badr. They planned to take back the money from the goods that had actually belonged to them. On one of the hottest days of summer, they set off from Medina. Because it was the month of Ramadan, the Companions were fasting. But since they were going into battle, the noble Prophet broke his fast and ordered everyone else to break their fasts to make it up later.

As the Muslims went toward Badr, they rode the camels in turns. When it was his turn to walk, the noble Prophet dismounted his camel. A nearby Companion couldn't stand him walking. He said, "O Messenger of Allah! You ride. We will walk instead of you."

The noble Prophet didn't accept the gesture. "You are not better than me at walking. And I am not less needy than you when it comes to being rewarded by Allah." And so he walked like the other Muslims.

Before the army of Islam reached the wells of Badr, Abu Sufyan heard of their approach. He immediately turned the caravan towards the Red Sea, and headed toward Mecca without passing Badr. Abu

Sufyan sent a messenger to Mecca, who shouted: "O people of Quraysh! They have attacked our trade caravan! Help now!"

The polytheists set off with approximately one thousand soldiers, who saw that the caravan was safe. But Abu Jahl didn't allow anyone to return.

The Messenger of Allah had prepared a small army intending only to intercept the caravan. He didn't want to do battle. But now the polytheists had prepared a large army, and were coming for them. The noble Prophet had a meeting with his Companions. He asked them whether to follow the caravan or do battle. At the end of the meeting, they decided to do battle.

How Many People Are There?

*B*attling the polytheists had been decided on. The army of Islam came close to the wells of Badr on a Friday night. The army of the polytheists from Mecca had encamped close to the wells of Badr, too. The blessed Prophet wanted to find out the number in the polytheist army. For this reason, he sent Ali ibn Abi Talib to the well.

Meanwhile, they caught one of the water bearers at the well and brought him back to camp. The Messenger of Allah spoke to the captured water bearer.

"Give me information about Quraysh."

"I swear by Allah, they are on the highest hill, on the furthest side of that dune."

"How many people are there?"

"Many."

"What could their number be?"

"I don't know!"

"How many camels do they slaughter each day?"

After thinking for a while the water bearer said, "Nine one day, and ten the other."

With this information, the noble Prophet said, "They are between 950 and 1000." By discovering the number of the polytheists, they reviewed their battle preparations. Then the blessed Prophet and his Companions went to the wells of Badr with their army.

They stored drinking water for themselves in a pool they made elsewhere. Then they closed the wells. The noble Prophet placed the army in position for battle. He checked the soldiers' positions, one by one. Then he gave directions to his army, "Do not leave your positions! Stay where you are without moving. Do not start the battle without my order. Do not waste your arrows before the enemy is near.

Use your swords at the end, when you are face to face with the enemy."

As the last preparations were being completed, the army of polytheists came. First, there were one-on-one clashes. In these clashes, Hamza ibn Abdul Muttalib and Ali ibn Abi Talib knocked down their opponents quickly. Then they helped Ubayda. But Ubayda had been wounded, and he was martyred that day.

There was a roar among the polytheists, who saw their soldiers being knocked down. Then they attacked. Full-on war began, with all its violence. At the end, the Muslims won a great victory. They gained a great number of spoils and slaves.

Among the prisoners were the blessed Prophet's cousins. The slaves' hands had been tied tightly so they couldn't escape. Hearing moans, the Messenger of Allah awakened in the middle of the night and couldn't sleep. His Companions saw he couldn't sleep and asked, "O Messenger of Allah! Why are you not sleeping?"

The beloved Prophet said, "Because of the moaning of Abbas." The Companions saw Allah's Messenger was upset and untied Abbas' hands.

When the moans ceased, the noble Prophet asked, "Why can't I hear Abbas moaning?"

They replied, "We untied him."

The Messenger of Allah said, "Untie all the slaves."

The slaves, untied, slept well that night.

Because there was no revelation about what should be done with the slaves, the noble Prophet had a meeting with his Companions. In the meeting, they decided that wealthy prisoners would be released in exchange for ransom. Literate prisoners who couldn't pay ransom were set free in exchange for teaching ten Muslims how to read. Illiterate and poor prisoners were set free.

Archers Hill

The Meccan polytheists wanted revenge for their defeat in the Battle of Badr, and to prevent Islam from spreading. So they established an army of three thousand men, and set forth without losing time.

Meanwhile, the noble Prophet had prepared an army of one thousand. It wasn't certain where the battle would take place.

The youth hoped to encounter the enemy outside the city, whereas the wise and experienced Companions wanted to stay in the city, for they felt defensive war would yield a better result.

But those who wanted to do battle outside the city were the majority. The noble Prophet complied with them, and together, they set off. They came as far as Mount Uhud. The two armies came face-to-face there.

The polytheists were arrogant because they were many. They had even brought entertainment to celebrate their victory.

The blessed Prophet organized his army in the best way. He pulled out his best fifty soldiers, and made them archers. He put Abdullah ibn Jubayr in charge of them. He wanted to send them to Aynayn Hill to secure the army's left and rear flanks. Hills to the right provided adequate cover.

To Abdullah ibn Jubayr, the beloved Prophet said, "Protect us with your arrows. Do not allow the cavalry near us. Don't let them strike from behind. Don't let the enemy strike from that direction. Do not leave your places, whether we win or lose the war."

Abdullah ibn Jubayr was an experienced soldier. He had been in the Battle of Badr, too.

Then the noble Prophet addressed the archers. He looked at them one by one. In a voice that everyone could hear, he said, "Protect our back well. Even if you see us being killed, do not leave your positions to come and help us. Even if you see us gathering spoils, do not come and join us. Even if you see us crush the enemy, do not leave your positions until I send you word."

The order was understood. The archers set off in great anticipation. In a short time, they had taken their positions on Aynayn Hill.

The battle started. From the first moment, it was clear how right the noble Prophet's decision was. The famous commander Khalid ibn Walid and his cavalry sought to attack the left flank of the army of Islam. But the soldiers on Aynayn Hill were masters of archery. They were shooting arrows at the enemy below, like fish in a barrel.

Khalid had to retreat. The army of Islam was bringing chaos to the polytheists. Khalid couldn't stand this scene. It was eating away at him. He gathered the cavalry and attacked again. The result was the same. Abdullah ibn Jubayr and his men were like a wall. It was impossible to get by them.

Polytheists had begun to flee. They were trying to save their own lives. Khalid charged once more. But they had to retreat without even reaching the army of Islam. Archer Hill wasn't merely shooting arrows, it was raining death on them. Khalid didn't give up. He made his soldiers wait.

There were no enemies left on the battlefield. They were all fleeing back to Mecca. They were so afraid, they didn't remember to pick up their flag from the ground. It seemed the Muslims had defeated the polytheists. Some soldiers had already started to gather the spoils left by the polytheists.

One of the archers cried out in joy, "We won! The war is over. Our men are gathering spoils. Let's go, too."

Abdullah ibn Jubayr was startled. Worried, he looked in Khalid's direction. He and his cavalry remained. Abdullah immediately called out to his soldiers. "Don't leave your positions! Didn't you hear the blessed Prophet's orders?"

But the archers were so thrilled at winning the battle that they started to run down the hill.

Astonished, Abdullah screamed after them, "Stop! Don't leave your positions! The war is not over yet!"

Those running down the hill didn't even hear him. Only a handful of archers remained.

Khalid noticed it right away. This was the opportunity he was looking for. He had been waiting for this moment. He turned to his cavalry and called out, "Attack!"

They all shot ahead together, like arrows. Shortly they reached Archer Hill. They slew those who remained. Then they attacked the army of Islam from behind. The army of Islam, which was chasing the enemy, stopped short when they heard screams from behind.

With his cavalry, Khalid plunged into the army of Islam with his sword high. The archers, busy gathering spoils, were stunned. They understood instantly what a big mistake they had made. But it was too late.

The polytheists who were fleeing returned when they saw Khalid attacking from behind. One of them picked up the flag. They started to do battle again. Now the Muslims were between two fires. They gathered around the Messenger of Allah. They risked their own lives to protect him. A thrown stone broke the blessed Prophet's tooth. The Companions built a wall of flesh around him. Exactly seventy Companions were martyred that day. The noble Prophet's dear uncle, Hamza ibn Abdul Muttalib, was among them.

The Muslims took refuge by a hill. The polytheists did not come any closer. They were afraid of turning their victory into defeat.

The polytheists returned joyfully to Mecca. They felt they owed their surprise victory to Khalid. They drank and made merry.

Just then, a messenger came to Abu Sufyan and the other leaders. Out of breath, he said, "Sir, the Muslims have recuperated. They are coming for us now with their remaining soldiers. By the looks of it, they want to catch up with us before we reach Mecca."

Abu Sufyan looked at the messenger in astonishment. It was hard to believe. How could the Muslims have recovered and made chase?

Suddenly, the polytheists were overwhelmed by fear. Abu Sufyan said, "We beat the Muslims once. But I don't know if we can do it again. It's best that we flee to Mecca in a hurry. Otherwise we will have to give back the victory we won!"

They moved quickly and reached Mecca in a short time. And so the Muslims had the upper hand once again.

Prophet Muhammad ﷺ

The Rock

a cavalryman rode his horse at a gallop in twilight. He reached Medina without resting. When he reached the streets of the city, everything looked normal. Merchants were selling their goods in the marketplace, and farmers were working in the fields. The messenger from the Huza'a tribe went directly to the noble Prophet.

"The Meccans are going to join forces with the Jews and attack Medina," he said.

The polytheists had prepared a large army, including neighboring tribes, and were coming for them. The messenger was shown a place to rest, and the noble Prophet gathered his Companions.

"Shall we battle out of Medina, or shall we stay in Medina and defend?" he asked.

After everyone shared their views, Salman al-Farisi offered, "O Messenger of Allah! When I was in Persia, we would dig trenches around us when we were afraid of enemy cavalry attacks."

This idea was accepted by the noble Prophet and his Companions. They immediately started to dig trenches around Medina.

The digging continued nonstop. But then the Companions came upon a hard rock. Whatever they did, they couldn't break it. They told Allah's Messenger.

The noble Prophet, who was resting in his tent, came to the rock. He took the sledgehammer in his hand and said, "In the Name of Allah." Then he hit the rock.

A part of the rock split off. The beloved Prophet said, "Allah is great! The keys of Damascus have been given to me. I swear to Allah that I see the red manors of Damascus." Then he said, "In the Name of Allah," and hit the rock with a sledgehammer.

Another part of the rock split off. "Allah is great! The keys of Persia have been given to me. I swear to

Allah that I see the city of Chosroes, and his white manors." For the third time he said, "In the Name of Allah," and hit the rock. The rest of the rock was broken. The noble Prophet said, "Allah is great! The keys of Yemen have been given to me. I swear to Allah that I see the gates of the city of Sana'a."

The rock was broken up and digging began again at full speed. Finally, the trenches were finished. Then the Muslims waited for the enemy.

When the army of polytheists saw the trenches, they didn't know what to do. Even their strongest horses could not cross the trenches. The war was stalled for days. One morning, by the permission of Allah, a strong sandstorm came in from the desert and caused disarray in the army of polytheists. The army had to give up and flee.

The Conquest of Mecca

The polytheists did not keep the promises they made at Hudaybiya. Before two years had passed, they attacked the Muslims, hence violating the Treaty of Hudaybiya. This was the straw that broke the camel's back. It was time for the real owners of Mecca to take it back. During these years of peace, the light of Islam had reached many places and the number of Muslims had increased considerably.

The number in the army of Islam was around ten thousand. Full of courage, Muslim soldiers came close to Mecca. They were going to spend the night there.

The most excited people in the army were the immigrants. They were returning to the homeland they had been ousted from. Heads high, and strong.

Abu Sufyan had heard about the army. He immediately set off with a few people. When he found the Messenger of Allah, he asked him for forgiveness.

Seeing the crowded army of Islam, Abu Sufyan made a choice. The light of Islam was dazzling. And so he made the declaration of faith, and became a Muslim himself.

Allah's Messenger said to his uncle Abbas, "Those who say 'There is no deity but the one and only Allah, and Muhammad is His servant and Messenger' are not to be touched. Those who enter their houses and close their doors are not to be touched. Those who leave their weapons and take refuge in the Ka'ba are not to be touched."

Abbas, may Allah be pleased with him, prepared to go and report this to the Meccans. To the noble Prophet, he said, "O Allah's Messenger, Abu Sufyan wants to return with me. Would you compliment him..."

Abu Sufyan could not take his eyes off the ground. He could not believe his life was being spared. But then the blessed Prophet conquered his heart, with a voice full of love.

"Those who take refuge in Abu Sufyan's house are not to be touched, either!"

The following day, while the army of Islam entered Mecca from all directions in an atmosphere of triumph, the noble Prophet was bent into two on top of his mount in modesty. He went straight to the Ka'ba. How he had been tortured and offended there years ago.

The people had gathered in the courtyard of the Ka'ba. There was hope and fear in their eyes. They were facing a man wrongfully exiled from his homeland, but he was also the beloved Prophet of mercy. Allah had sent him as a "mercy for all the worlds." With his hands, the Messenger of Allah knocked down the idols one by one to return the Ka'ba to its original purity. Then he turned to the people.

"What do you expect I will do to you?" he asked.

They answered, "We ask for goodness and expect goodness from you. You are a merciful cousin. You are strong."

The Messenger of Allah looked Meccans over carefully from one end to the other, and said, "I say to you what Prophet Joseph said to his brothers. '*No reproach this day shall be on you, and no taunting.*' Go all of you, you are all free!"

At these words, the people burst into tears of relief and joy. The doors of their houses opened one by one. People ventured forth confidently. The blessed Prophet had conquered Mecca, and their hearts. One by one, they made the declaration of faith, and became Muslims. In the year 630, the winds of happiness were blowing in Mecca.

The Farewell Pilgrimage

The noble Prophet was taking his pilgrimage. He performed *tawaf* around the Ka'ba. Then he started to pray at Safa Hillock.

Meanwhile Muslims flowed into Mecca. Their number passed one hundred thousand.

The Messenger of Allah mounted his camel. He came to the place called Arafat. The Muslims gathered there. Everybody was looking at his lips, waiting breathlessly for his words. Finally, Allah's Messenger began to speak. "O my people. Listen to me carefully. I don't know if I will be able to see you again after this year..."

The Messenger of Allah said many beautiful things in his Farewell Sermon. At the end, he looked out at everyone and said, "O my people. They will ask you about me. What will you say?"

Thousands of people cried out together. "We will say he did his duty duly!"

The blessed Prophet looked up to the sky. He raised his right index finger and said, "Witness this, O my Lord. Witness this, O my Lord. Witness this, O my Lord!"

At that moment, the noble Prophet recited the verse that had just come from Allah Almighty. *"This day I have perfected for you your religion (with all its rules, commandments and universality), completed My favor upon you, and have been pleased to assign for you Islam as your religion."*

At that moment, someone in the crowd started to cry. It was no other than the blessed Prophet's closest friend, Abu Bakr.

Abu Bakr knew that Allah's Messenger was going to leave them. This pilgrimage was his farewell pilgrimage.

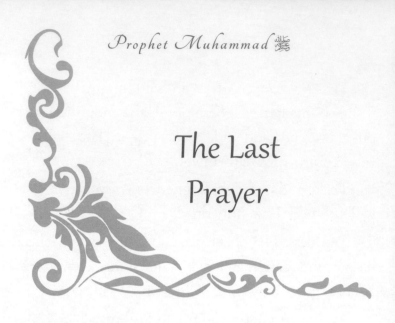

The Last Prayer

The beloved Prophet fell ill one day, when he was sixty-three years old. He had a severe headache.

Aisha, may Allah be pleased with her, never left the beloved Prophet alone. She was feeling his pain in her own heart. She was ceaselessly praying to Allah, for His Messenger.

His illness went on for about two weeks. During this time, the noble Prophet's pain didn't ease at all.

One day, as the time for the Night Prayer was approaching, he passed out. Aisha was very sad. In tears, she started to pray again.

When the Messenger of Allah, peace and blessings be upon him, regained consciousness, he turned to his wife Aisha and said, "Has the Prayer started?" Trying not to show the tears in her eyes, she answered, "No, they are waiting for you."

The Companions were waiting for the noble Prophet to lead the Prayer, as he always did. They were watching the door. They knew he was going to walk through that door soon, with a smile on his face, stand in front of them, and lead the Prayer once again. As he always did.

But not this time. The door did not open.

The Messenger of Allah said to Aisha, "Tell Abu Bakr that he should lead the Prayers." Aisha couldn't hold back anymore. She began to cry. With a trembling voice, she said, "O Messenger of Allah! My father is a very sentimental person. He always cries when he recites the Qur'an. He couldn't stand taking your place and leading the Prayers."

The blessed Prophet insisted, "Tell Abu Bakr. He shall lead the Prayers!"

She tried the same answer again. But the noble Prophet didn't change his mind.

"Tell Abu Bakr. He shall lead the Prayers!"

Aisha did as she was told. She gave the noble Prophet's order to her father.

For a moment, Abu Bakr didn't know what to say. As soon as he pulled himself together, he turned to Umar ibn al Khattab, may Allah be pleased with them both. "O Umar. Could you lead the Prayers..."

Umar shook his head and said, "No, no! O Abu Bakr, you are more worthy for this than me!"

A little while later, Abu Bakr, in his touching voice, was reciting Allah's verses in the mosque. The Messenger of Allah was listening to him from his room. Abu Bakr was crying, the Companions behind him were crying, Aisha was crying...

Prophet Muhammad ﷺ

The Reunion

It was a Monday. The noble Prophet's illness had become unbearable. But he never complained at all. To cope with his pain, he prayed to Allah, "O Lord of people. Resolve difficulties. Give healing. You are the true Healer. You are the only One Who takes away problems!"

At one stage, he started to feel all right. He got up. His face was pale from his illness.

He managed to walk to the door and look into the mosque. The Companions' eyes met his own. At that moment, everybody felt joyful. They were excited to see the blessed Prophet on his feet.

Right away, Abu Bakr abandoned the position of *imam*. He moved aside and invited the blessed Prophet to lead the Prayer. Everybody wanted the Messenger of Allah to lead the Prayers again.

Our Prophet smiled slightly. Looking straight into their eyes he said, "Come on, complete your Prayer."

Then he went back to his room, and lay down in the bed he had just left. Hearts were filled with sorrow once again in the mosque.

The Messenger of Allah was repeating the same prayer continuously. "O Lord of people! Resolve difficulties. Give healing. You are the true Healer. You are the only One Who takes away problems!"

Aisha was waiting at the noble Prophet's side. She couldn't take her eyes off him for even a moment. She held his hand. His illness had gotten worse. They stayed like that for a long while. Then Aisha raised her hands to pray for the blessed Prophet to get better. But the Messenger of Allah pulled his hand back slightly and said his last words: "Forgive me, Allah! Accept me to Your Exalted Friendship and Company. Dear Lord! I want Your Exalted Friendship!"

The noble Prophet who was mercy for all the worlds was now in Allah's merciful hands.

Sorrow

The word that Allah's Messenger had died started a storm in the hearts of the people. The Companions didn't know what to do. Nobody spoke. It was as if everyone was frozen. Umar was staring into the distance. Uthman had collapsed where he was. Ali was unconscious, as if he had been hit by something.

Umar jumped to his feet, all of a sudden. He had pulled out his sword. He looked at everyone there and screamed, at the top of his voice, "I will kill whoever says Muhammad has died!"

Nobody was in a state to hear him. Everybody was looking at a point, just like a statue.

Then Abu Bakr came in. The Messenger of Allah was wrapped in white cloth.

Abu Bakr slightly pulled the cover off the noble Prophet's face. He looked on for some time. He murmured, "You were beautiful alive, and you are beautiful dead!" Then he kissed the beloved Prophet's face. And tears fell from his eyes.

He heard Umar's loud voice outside. "I swear to Allah, the Prophet didn't die! The Messenger of Allah didn't die!"

Abu Bakr slowly stood up and walked outside. He looked at the Muslims, and turned to Umar, saying: "Sit, O Umar."

But Umar was beside himself. He didn't even hear Abu Bakr.

So Abu Bakr turned to the people there and said, "O people! Whoever believes in Muhammad should know that he is dead. Whoever believes in Allah should know that He is the All-Alive and will never die!"

Umar began to come to his senses. His hands fell to his sides. Abu Bakr finished his words with a verse from the Qur'an. *"Muhammad is only a Prophet! And Prophets passed away before him. If, then, he dies or is killed, will you turn back on your heels?"*

When Umar heard this verse, he collapsed. He had fainted. When he regained consciousness, he was calm.

The Muslims had to accept the situation. In the end, the Messenger of Allah was a human, too. Like every other living creature, he would taste death. Only Allah is immortal.

They started the preparations to bury the blessed Prophet. A few people, lead by Ali ibn Abi Talib, washed his blessed body. They wrapped him with three layers of cloth. They enshrouded him in Yemeni cloth.

Then a discussion started. They couldn't decide where to bury the blessed Prophet. Everyone had a different opinion. Abu Bakr came forward and said, "I heard the noble Prophet say, 'All Prophets were buried where they died!'"

The discussion was over. The beloved Prophet's grave was dug right there. Before long, his blessed body was placed in the soil.